Makers of Kenya's History

Joseph Daniel Otiende

Makers of Kenya's History
SERIES EDITOR: PROF. SIMIYU WANDIBBA

1. *Jomo Kenyatta*	Eric M. Aseka
2. *Ronald Ngala*	Eric M. Aseka
3. *Nabongo Mumia*	Simon Kenyanchui
4. *Dedan Kimathi*	Tabitha Kanogo
5. *Tom Mboya*	Edwin Gimode
6. *Masinde Muliro*	Simiyu Wandibba
7. *Elijah Masinde*	Vincent G. Simiyu
8. *Jaramogi Oginga Odinga*	E.S. Atieno-Odhiambo
9. *J.M. Kariuki*	Simiyu Wandibba
10. *Olonana ole Mbatian*	Peter Ndege
11. *Alibhai Mulla Jeevanjee*	Zarina Patel
12. *Wangu wa Makeri*	Mary W. Wanyoike
13. *Joseph Daniel Otiende*	Peter Wanyande

Makers of Kenya's History

JOSEPH DANIEL OTIENDE

Peter Wanyande

EAST AFRICAN EDUCATIONAL PUBLISHERS
Nairobi • Kampala • Dar es Salaam

Published by
East African Educational Publishers Ltd.
Brick Court, Mpaka Road/Woodvale Grove
Westlands, P.O. Box 45314
Nairobi

East African Educational Publishers Ltd.
P.O. Box 11542
Kampala

Ujuzi Educational Publishers Ltd.
P.O. Box 31647, Kijito-Nyama
Dar es Salaam

© Peter Wanyande 2002

First published 2002

ISBN 9966-25-156-1

Cover Illustration by John Nyagah
Photo sections courtesy of J.D. Otiende

Printed by Kenya Litho Ltd.
Changamwe Road, P.O. Box 40775, Nairobi

DEDICATION

To my late parents;
Norbert Odiwuor and Catherine Ochol,
for their support.

CONTENTS

Preface .... *ix*

Acknowledgement .... *xi*

Chapter 1: Childhood, Education and Training 1

Chapter 2: Otiende the Teacher and Administrator 8

Chapter 3: Early Political Activities 15

Chapter 4: The East Africa Common Services Organisation 28

Chapter 5: Independence and After 31

Chapter 6: Life After Active Politics 48

Chapter 7: Conclusion 63

Bibliography 65

PREFACE

The attainment of independence stands out as one of the most important achievements in the political history of Kenya. The event helped restore the dignity and pride of Kenyans after over seventy years of humiliation and servitude by the colonial government. The achievement was possible through the courage, dedication and visionary leadership of a handful of Kenyans who practised self-denial in order to free their countrymen and women from the cruel and brutal colonial bondage. Their role ought to inspire Kenyans to rededicate themselves to the ideals for which these brave Kenyans fought for, namely *Uhuru*.

These same Kenyans, appropriately referred to as Nationalists, went on to lay the foundation for nation building after independence. Joseph Daniel Otiende was one such nationalist who risked and sacrificed a lot to fight against colonial rule. His role was however not confined to direct battle for independence. As a teacher during the colonial period, Otiende helped mould the future of many Kenyans who went on to contribute to national development in different capacities. He was also involved in developing the local government system when he served in the then North Nyanza Council. As a minister in the first independent government, Otiende laid the foundation for the education and health sectors. Otiende performed his duties with a lot of interest, dedication and vision. He toured every part of the country to familiarise himself with problems affecting the various ministries he headed. Otiende also served in the East African Legislative Council as a minister, a portfolio he took charge of with distinction.

This book captures his role and contribution to the struggle for independence and nation building after *Uhuru*. Otiende must also be respected for being one of the few nationalists who shunned corruption. He lives a simple but joyous life in this village and receives visitors from all walks of life - local and foreign - who come to seek his opinion and advice on a number of issues. He must also be respected for being among the few politicians who willingly and voluntarily gave up politics when he thought the time had come. He has shown that one can serve one's country even after retiring from active politics. Many politicians therefore have a lot to learn from this son of Maragoli.

Prof. Peter Wanyande
University of Nairobi
June 2002

ACKNOWLEDGEMENT

This work has benefited from several individuals. First I wish to thank Professor Simiyu Wandibba, the Series Editor for giving me an opportunity to conduct research on and write a book about Otiende's role in the struggle for independence and his contribution to nation building. Secondly I wish to thank Mzee Joseph Otiende himself, the subject of this publication, for the valuable information and insights he gave me on his role in the nationalist struggle, as well as about this country - both during the colonial and postcolonial periods. I also thank him for trusting me with his treasured photographs that have formed the photo-sections of this book.

My sincere thanks also go to Rose Tamoo, my Research Assistant, for the library research she carried out that generated some of the data on Otiende's role in the struggle for independence and after. Rose also typed several versions of the manuscript.

Finally I wish to thank my wife Serrah, daughter Katherine Adhiambo, and son James Ratego for the support and encouragement they gave me throughout the duration of this project.

J.D. Otiende in a pensive mood. He is a self-effacing politician.

CHAPTER ONE

CHILDHOOD, EDUCATION AND TRAINING

Family background

Joseph Daniel Otiende comes from the Avaloogoli sub-nation of the larger Abaluyia community. The Abaluyia are divided into seventeen sub-nations, each of which is a union of several clans living in a continuous territory. A sub-nation is distinguished by its dialect and its special customs. Abaluyia sub-nations include Abanyore, Abasamia, Babukusu, Abatirichi, Avaloogoli, Abamarachi, Abawanga, Abashisa, Abanyala (Navakholo), Abanyala (Port Victoria), Abakabras, Abatachoni, Abeisukha, Abeidakho, Abakhayo, Abatura and Abatsotso. Each of these sub-nations is further divided into a number of clans. The Avaloogoli, for example, are divided into four clans, namely, Abasali, Abakizungu, Abakirima and Abamaabi. In their story of origin, migration and settlement, these people claim to have come from 'Misri', which could mean either Egypt or the general area north of Mount Elgon.

Otiende, Omuloogoli, was the eldest child of Mzee Daniel Akelo and Mama Abigael Irangi of Kegoye village in present day Vihiga District. The district was recently curved out of the larger Kakamega District. The other districts that were recently curved out of the original Kakamega District are Butere-Mumias and Malava-Lugari.

Otiende had one brother and seven sisters. He gives his birthday as 21st September 1917. This makes him 84 years old at the time this study was conducted. At the time of his birth, little did anyone know that the little boy would make an outstanding contribution in the struggle for the independence of this country and, later, in the initial stages of nation building. Being the oldest child in his family, and a son for that matter, Otiende had the responsibility of looking after his younger brothers and sisters. His parents expected him to set a good example to the rest of the children, a challenge he believes he lived up to.

Otiende began schooling at the tender age of 7 years, thanks to his father and the community in general who understood the value of education. His father was a teacher who later became a priest. Mzee Akelo is also known for having started schools in his area. While in most parts of the country colonialists were held with a lot of suspicion, different attitudes existed among the people of Western Kenya about the possible benefits of associating with the foreigners. The majority of these people were open to overtures. Their leaders often approached missionary explorers and gave them gifts while begging them to settle nearby and start schools. This explains the high number of missionary schools in Western Kenya compared to other regions. The Church Missionary Society (CMS) missionaries, who arrived in the country in 1890s, settled in Mbale, Uganda, which at that time was part of the present day Kenya. The CMS had branches in Butere and Maseno. Friends African Mission settled in Kaimosi. In 1902 the CMS were ordered by the governor to move to Vihiga. The CMS then moved to Maseno in 1905. However, due to the suspicion and the subsequent hostility of the Nandi towards foreigners – that later led to the famous Nandi war between the British and the Nandi which ended in 1905 – the Friends African Mission settled in Kaimosi and later Maseno, where they started the prestigious Maseno School in 1908. Maseno was then part of Kisumu District. In 1905 the Anglican Missionaries moved to Vihiga. Later in 1921, they established Butere Normal School, which Otiende joined in 1925 in Standard One. He was a boarder. In 1926 Butere Normal School was merged with Maseno School under CMS. Later Butere Normal School became a Teacher Training College.

Other schools opened by missionaries around the same time include St. Mary's Yala, which was started by Catholic Missionaries, and Kaimosi, which was started by Friends African Mission (FAM) missionaries. These schools were established mainly to cater for boys' education.

Unlike many African children of the time who did not go to school, Otiende was lucky because his father Mzee Daniel Akelo was a beneficiary of these missionary schools. Akelo had been educated in Kisumu where he had spent most of his early life. In fact, he got his name Akelo from Luoland. Mzee Akelo later worked for Chief Adhola, the then chief of Asembo before he moved back to Maseno in 1910 as a teacher. He taught for several years and also started several schools around his home area. He later started studying the Bible and preaching, quit teaching and became a priest. Since Mzee Akelo was also good at many local languages such as Dholuo, Kalenjin and Teso, he used this to translate the Bible and church services to the local people. Otiende also learnt many local languages. Apart from his own, he is fluent in Dholuo, Gikuyu, Kalenjin and even Luganda.

Education

Having known the value of Western education, Mzee Akelo took his children to school. However, even before the introduction of Western education, African children were not left in total ignorance. There was in place a system of education that Otiende jokingly refers to as "bush" school. By 1924, Otiende had undergone this traditional form of education. Traditional education was seen as preparation for living in the society in which one was born; an education that was strongly adapted to the environment and aimed at conserving the cultural heritage of the family, clan and the community in general. Otiende was taught that his future and that of the community depended on the continuation and understanding of their ethnic institutions of law, language, customs and values that they had inherited from the past. Through this form of education the youth were exposed to, and socialised into, the ways of the community. It was an informal kind of education in which learning was by storytelling and sometimes by role-playing. The education was conducted mainly in the evening and the teachers were the elders of the community. Otiende observes that one of the major differences between this kind of education and the Western one is the fact that it was accessible to everyone in the community. This is because, he says, students did not pay fees. There were also no dropouts as the time for school was usually convenient to the learners.

Disruption of informal education, Otiende says, has been brought about by two developments in this country. The first is the coming of the Europeans and their determination to replace African values with Western ones. Otiende remembers being told by the White teachers to embrace the Western ways of doing things in the place of the African or traditional ways. Education, religion and medicine were some of the areas most affected. A number of parents, he says, followed this and discouraged their children from participating in traditional education. The second major development to which Otiende attributes the erosion of traditional education is urbanisation, which he also associates with the coming of the white man. Urbanisation has led to the migration of people from rural into the urban areas and this has resulted in the acquisition of new values. Indeed, Otiende laments that the new values have caused the youth and Africans in general to abandon their indigenous ways. In any case, the youth no longer value the rural areas where the majority of people live. Otiende says he is happy that he was adequately exposed to the urban and rural life alike. He nolstagically remembers how peaceful rural life was during his childhood. In Asembo and Maragoli villages where he grew up people respected each other. They were very friendly and children were regarded as belonging to the community. Any adult could ask a child to undertake a task regardless of whose child it was. Adult relatives were allowed to discipline children even in the absence of their parents. This, he laments, does not happen anymore, especially in the urban areas.

His strong belief in the value of education perhaps explains why he gave the best education to his children.

In 1924, Otiende joined Kagoye Primary School in his home area. It was here that for the first time, he came face to face with a white man. It was here that he saw, also for the first time, a Black man speaking American English, earning himself the nickname "black American". This man's name was Dr. Aggrey Kwegyire, who had been invited from South Africa to study how African education could be improved. According to Otiende, Dr. Aggrey made a very great impression on Kenyans.

Otiende was later sent to a boarding school, the Butere Boarding Vocational School in 1925. From Butere, Otiende moved to Maseno in 1926 where he remained up to 1929. Maseno was a great experience for Otiende. He rubbed shoulders with a lot of people who later became prominent in the country. For instance, he remembers his classmates who included Oginga Odinga, who later became the first Vice-President of independent Kenya, one of the first African DCs, Mr. Okwiri Jusa, retired Archbishop Festus Olang' and Walter Odede among others. He says he became a close friend of Oginga Odinga and this had great influence on his later decision to join politics, a subject discussed in detail elsewhere in this booklet.

Otiende sat for secondary school examination in Maseno and joined Alliance High School in 1930. He was the first person from his village to join Alliance, an achievement that put him in the limelight. Then, like now, Alliance was a very prestigious school that only admitted the very best. It was very competitive. Little wonder that back home he became the 'village hero' and the elders were really proud of him. At Alliance he had the chance to meet, study and mingle with people from different communities who included the late Jackson Angaine, Isaac Okwiri and the late James Gichuru. Angaine, Gichuru and Otiende later served in different capacities in the Kenyan cabinet after the country attained independence. Interaction with many different people changed Otiende's view of ethnicity and tribal backgrounds as he started valuing people as Kenyans rather than Abaluyia or Luo. He learnt to appreciate other communities and look at their problems like they were his own. From this, he developed an attitude that later became an asset in his political life – that of service to the people irrespective of their ethnic backgrounds.

One of the things that baffles Otiende about the contemporary Kenyan society is the fact that even though people are now exposed to the existence of many ethnic groups, they prefer to glorify their differences rather than their similarities. He detests people's tendency to emphasize their ethnic origins at a time when unity is needed most. This, he contends, was not pronounced during the pre-independence days. If it had been that way, he says, the country would not have achieved independence at the time it did. Nationalism was very strong during the struggle for independence. People united to get rid of the colonial rulers despite the numerous political and legal obstructions that were placed in the way to block this goal. He laments that nowadays people find it difficult to unite even against a common enemy such as poverty. In his opinion, failure to unite is one of the biggest problems of our times.

Towards Otiende's completion of secondary education, the colonial government began an experiment to see how Africans could perform at higher levels of education. They introduced a Makerere Entrance Examination, known as the Senior Cambridge Certificate. Otiende was in the trial group. Being the bright young man he was, he sat for the examination and passed well enough to proceed for higher education. He was among the first Kenyans, including James Gitau Kanyua and James Gichuru, to join the then Makerere College in Kampala, Uganda. Makerere was the only University College in East and Central Africa and therefore, very competitive. At Makerere Otiende tried the medical discipline for a few months but later quit to study education. His decision was influenced by the elders of his community. They had wanted Otiende to become a teacher and were unhappy when they learnt that he was studying medicine. They consequently prevailed upon him to quit and join the faculty of education. Otiende says that he did not at that time understand why his community wanted him to study education and become a teacher rather than a doctor. He, however, did not question the position taken by the elders as this would have been unbecoming. Looking back, however, he thinks that the reason had to do with the high esteem by which the white teachers were regarded by the community. They wanted their son to be like the white man. Apparently, the community had not interacted with a white doctor and so the idea was remote to them. Otiende expresses disappointment at the fact that teachers are no longer accorded the kind of respect that befits the teaching profession. He says this is one of the things that Kenyans should pay attention to as we try to improve education in the country. Otiende also reasons that since the community had enough medicinemen, they did not wish him to train as a doctor.

It must be noted, however, that Otiende's interest in medicine did not diminish after settling for a course in education. He still has an interest in medicine and engages in the practice of traditional medicine.

CHAPTER TWO

OTIENDE THE TEACHER AND ADMINISTRATOR

After completing his studies at Makerere, Otiende was posted to Kaimosi Mission in Western Province in 1937 to run its intermediate school. This was one of the few schools for Africans in Western Province and he remembers how the schools were far apart. This was because the colonial government did not place a very high premium on African education. Indeed, most schools during this period, Otiende says, were owned by the Christian missionaries, notably the CMS and Catholic missionaries. A few were also owned by the Seventh Day Adventists (SDA). These schools included St. Mary's Yala, Maseno High School, Kaimosi Mission School and a few others. Each religious group, including the Catholics and the Protestants, had its own schools. This was complicated by the racial discrimination in the education system. There were schools for Europeans, Indians and Africans. Otiende speaks very positively about the Christian missionaries for their role in providing education to this country.

Being his first time to teach, Otiende says that his first posting as a teacher was a very big challenge. He wanted to prove himself because he realised that if he did not do so, the white man would consider the job too demanding for a black man. He was, therefore, determined to succeed and in his opinion, he did, during his tenure at Kaimosi. He thinks it was his success that earned him a transfer to Alliance High School two years later.

At Alliance, Otiende replaced Eliud Mathu who was proceeding abroad for further studies. At this time European teachers dominated the school. The only African teachers were Mathu, Gichuru and later Otiende. At Alliance he says he taught academic giants like Professor Simeon Ominde, Professor David Wasawo, Professor Morris Alala and Ezekiel Minjo. Others included Jeremiah Nyagah, Julius Gikonyo Kiano, Paul Ngei and Njoroge Mungai. Most of these became politicians who played an active role in the struggle for independence. Nyagah, Kiano, Ngei and Mungai became cabinet ministers in the first post-colonial government. Others like Simeon Ominde and David Wasawo became university professors. He remembers Wasawo as one of the brightest students even recognised by the European teachers especially Carey Francis, the headmaster of Alliance High School at that time. In this regard, Otiende is proud to be associated with developing and moulding of such prominent Kenyans. He is quite happy to see most of his former students occupying key positions in the government and in other local and international organisations.

Otiende remained a teacher at Alliance for eight years before he was transferred to Jeans School, Kabete (now Kenya Institute of Administration) under Colonel Blundell who was then the head of the department of Social Welfare and Rehabilitation. The school was established by the British after the Second World War as a reward for Kenyans' contribution and support for Britain. During this war, the British had performed very poorly against the Germans. They were forced to come for reinforcement from Africa, Kenya included. This saw many Kenyans participate in the war, most of them as carriers of ammunitions and other supplies required by the British soldiers who were fighting in the war. The pioneer corps were those people who prepared the roads for the army during the 1939/45 war. They were locally refered to as *Panyako*. When the war ended, the colonial government decided that something positive had to be done for these men in order to help them improve their lives. Jeans School was thus created as a deliberate attempt by the colonial government to uplift the lives of those men who fought in the war. Otiende was responsible for training these ex-army men to help them adapt to civilian life. He has not forgotten the joy of teaching adults who had experienced the "real" world. It was particularly interesting to hear them narrate their experiences. Africans later used their contribution to the war as a base on which to negotiate for better treatment from the whites. The experience also raised their level of political consciousness which slowly bore the independence struggle and eventually independence. Thus, even though Otiende condemns the recruitment of Africans, and Kenyans in particular, to fight in a war they did not cause, he thinks it made a positive contribution. He is of the opinion that nationalism was given a new impetus by these experiences.

Most graduates of the Jeans School later became important people in this country. Moses Mudavadi who became a teacher, an education officer and later joined politics – rising to the position of cabinet minister under President Moi's government – is one of them.

The Local Native Council

It was during Otiende's teaching stint at Jeans School that senior officers from the African Council of North Nyanza approached him and requested him to run for the Local Native Council (LNC). Among the officers were Chief Henry Kere, Chief William Shivachi, Paramount Chief Hezron Buyoywa and Chief Jonathan Barasa. The LNCs were established by the colonial Legislative Council (LEGCO) in 1924 through enactment of the Native Authority (Amendment) Ordinance. Ordinances were the equivalent of present day Acts of Parliament. The 1924 Ordinance was an amendment of the Local Authority Ordinance passed in 1912. This Ordinance laid the foundation for a local government system for Africans by providing the legal framework for it. Prior to this, only areas where the Europeans settled were governed by a local authority – the precursor to the present day local authorities.

The objectives of the Local Native Councils included the following:
a) To encourage a sense of responsibility and duty towards the state among the chiefs and elders and among the more thoughtful of the native population.
b) To provide the younger and educated Africans with a definite avenue along which to develop.
c) To provide a voice to the educated native and avenue for expression of his aspirations.
d) To provide an avenue for complaints so that the government could understand the people's needs.

In line with these responsibilities, the local government authorities had their own sources of revenue and institutions such as local courts, schools and health centres. According to Otiende, during the colonial period the Local Councils were fully autonomous entities. For instance, the council could send people abroad for further studies without having to go through the central government. Furthermore, all district basic services were under councils and not the central government. The councils collected their own revenue and provided services to the people, managing to save millions of shillings every year. The services they provided included education, health, roads, and cleanliness. Otiende asserts that the councils then were more effective as far as provision of services was concerned than they are now. Thus, to run a council was quite prestigious. It was also very challenging. This influenced his decision to accept the request from senior officers from the African Council of North Nyanza. He thought he could serve his people better and more effectively from this position. Service to the people, he said, had become his major objective in life. Otiende feels that today the central government has too much power over the local authorities, to the extent that their autonomy has been compromised. The problem, according to him, is that the central government is bent on monopolising power. This is achieved by weakening institutions such as local authorities that have the potential to provide an independent power base for politicians at the local level. The government's reluctance to amend the Local Government Act Cap 265 is testimony to this, he asserts. The Act gives the minister for local government, and therefore the central government, too much power over the local authorities. This is one major explanation of the poor provision of services by these authorities. The only remedy, Otiende suggests, is to relieve the central government of some of the powers it has over the local authorities. It needs to be pointed out here that the central government control over local government started as early as 1969 when some major functions then performed by the local authorities were transferred to the central government. Among the powers and functions that were transferred were the provision of primary education, health services and roads. The transfer of these functions was effected after the introduction or enactment of the Local Government (Transfer of Functions) Act 1969. The Act gave the president power to amend existing Acts to facilitate the transfer of a number of administration services from the local government. The justification for transferring these functions was that the local authorities were not performing these services efficiently due to limited funds. Their main source of revenue had been the Graduated Personal Tax (GPT) which had been introduced in 1963. The revenue was, however, not sufficient to pay for the services provided by local authorities. The abolition of the GPT by the central government further undermined the financial strength of local authorities.

Otiende observes that local authorities are now a pale shadow of what they were in colonial times. The economic strength of many local authorities has also been undermined in the recent past by the creation of many local authorities that are not economically viable. A number of local authorities have also been upgraded without due consideration of their ability to provide the services that go with the new status. The original Kiambu County Council, for example, has been split into Thika County Council, Thika Municipal Council, Ruiru Municipal Council and Limuru Town Council, thereby effectively reducing the economic strength of the original Kiambu County

Council. The five councils now have to share the resources that hitherto belonged to Kiambu County Council. Similarly, the creation of Ukwala Town Council without due regard to its ability to raise revenue has led to a situation in which, on several occasions, the council has been unable to pay salaries to its workers. It would appear that the creation of these councils that are not economically viable is driven mainly by political considerations.

Otiende accepted the offer to run the LNC and this marked the end of his teaching career, which he had enjoyed very much. He joined the council as the Assistant Clerk to the African District Council (ADC). At the council, he was responsible for the general development of the district. He controlled a special fund known as the 'African Betterment Fund'. This was a fund that could be used to undertake special development projects for the Africans. The colonial system was racially segregated and each race had its own development projects. Otiende's responsibility was basically to ensure the development of the area under the jurisdiction of his council. While at the ADC, Otiende, who always had the interest of fellow Africans at heart, realised that farmers around Kimilili were experiencing poor harvests, a condition he attributed to land overuse which had led to infertility of the soil. He therefore organised trucks to ferry compost manure to this region. He also undertook the initiative of educating the local people on how to use manure and its importance in agriculture and the response was extremely positive. Otiende gladly remembers how his effort paid off when yields increased appreciably and though they were not quantified, it was certain the farmers did well in terms of yields after this.

Working for the LNC gave Otiende enormous experience which later proved invaluable to his political career. To start with, it enabled him to tour most of the area. He thus knew the place quite well. This proved useful when he became the Member of Parliament for Vihiga constituency. He knew all the thirty-seven clans in his constituency and this helped his work as an MP. He points out that it was very easy for him to obtain information about the needs of his constituency from the clan elders, in spite of the large area his constituency covered. When later he joined the cabinet, he made a point of touring the entire country. This enabled him to determine where to build facilities such as health centres and hospitals. Otiende expresses his disappointment at the fact that these days many ministers do not tour some parts of the country. They do not seem to realise that as cabinet ministers they have a duty to the whole country. He laments that many MPs do not know their constituencies well and thus do not understand the development needs in different parts of their constituencies – which is quite unfortunate.

CHAPTER THREE

EARLY POLITICAL ACTIVITIES

The Land Issue

Otiende's interest in active politics may have started when he was a young man in his mid-20s. In the early 1930s, gold was discovered in Kakamega, which subsequently led to the so-called Kakamega gold rush. The Europeans rushed to the region with the aim of prospecting for this precious mineral. Sensing the danger of being displaced, the local residents requested potential miners to sign an agreement that they would leave once the prospecting was over, a request the Europeans vehemently refused to accept. Thus, this gold rush and the corresponding threat of land alienation in North Nyanza led to the establishment of the North Kavirondo Association by the local people, to oppose the alienation of land. This Association was similar to the Kikuyu Central Association (KCA) which was formed in 1924 by Joseph Kang'ethe and James Beauttah to protest against the alienation of Gikuyu land. KCA had called for the repeal of the Crown Lands Ordinance of 1915, which had turned Africans into tenants at the will of the Crown. More disturbing to Otiende was the fact that the Africans were tenants in their own country. The Kikuyu Central Association also protested the ban on growing of cash crops by Africans. In the Central Province of Kenya, some of the best African land had been alienated for European use, thus limiting Africans' agricultural production. The Europeans owned most of the large-scale farming production and the best and richest land of the Kenya Highlands, while the Africans lived in crowded reserves as peasants relying only on subsistence farming. The formation of KCA was intended to persuade the colonial government to ensure that land was also made available to the Africans.

At the time of the Kakamega gold rush, Otiende was a student at Alliance High School from where he was exposed to the issue of land. White settlers had already alienated much of Gikuyu land leading to the formation of KCA. To show solidarity with his fellow Kenyans, Otiende became a junior member of KCA. To him it did not matter that he was a Luyia and not a Gikuyu. All that mattered was that fellow Kenyans' land had been taken away. Even during those early days, Otiende did not have tribal chauvinism. He believed people were meant to fight as Kenyans rather than being divided along ethnic lines. While a member of KCA, he was among those who championed the rights of the Africans, especially the right to own land. It was, therefore, not surprising that when the Europeans began to control the gold fields in Kakamega, Otiende saw an opportunity to mobilise the affected people to resist the move.

Events taking place outside the colony may also have propelled Otiende into joining active politics. Such events include the Ethiopian war of 1935. The invasion of Eritrea by the Italians angered many Africans. It dawned on them that the presence of the white man meant trouble for the Africans and that they had to do something about it. This invasion acted as an eye opener to many Africans. They felt they had a duty to fight against invasion of their country by the colonialists.

The Birth of Nationalism

The Great War of 1939, later dubbed the Second World War, worsened the situation. The Second World War had a very significant effect on the political climate of Kenya. This is the war in which very many Africans, Kenyans included, were taken to fight on the British side.

Those who did not actually fight, were used as carriers, cooks, etc. However, the experience they obtained from this war was the same. Apart from gaining fighting experience, the Africans also came to know that the white man was not special in any way. Not only did Europeans get injured like their African counterparts, but very many of them were killed alongside the blacks. This experience gave Africans a new perspective of looking at the white man, who they had earlier regarded as superhuman. They realised that they too could fight him. For Otiende and others who did not fight in the war, they heard about the experiences from those who did, and similarly concluded that the European was not any special and had to leave. This, together with the guerrilla tactics Africans learnt while fighting the Japanese, contributed greatly to the spirit of nationalism that emerged among Africans after the Second World War. Africans began organising themselves into political parties through which they could air their grievances to the colonial government. Otiende says organisations such as Pan Africanism gave a lot of encouragement to the budding nationalist movements in Kenya and other African countries. Nationalists such the late President Jomo Kenyatta and Nnamdi Azikiwe were active members of the Pan African movement.

However, fearing that Africans might rise against them, the colonial administration proscribed all political parties and forced their leaders into detention camps. Otiende refers to this period as most trying for the nationalists. The idea behind these detentions, he says, was to instil fear among the nationalists. This, however, did not deter political activism among the blacks. Instead there arose an increased African sensitivity and aspiration as more and more African ex-servicemen returned home from the war. These ex-servicemen had high economic and political awareness, especially as they faced the serious problems of unemployment and overcrowding. They had also interacted with Europeans in their own countries and learnt a lot about them. They understood their strengths and weaknesses. They argued that the Europeans had no right to enjoy certain things which they denied other people. In any case what the Africans were fighting for was not different from what the Europeans had achieved in their own countries.

Otiende, being among the few Africans that had received Western education, joined other educated elites at the national level to provide a new strategy for political leadership. With their educational background, they were clearly aware of the injustices of the colonial administration against fellow Africans. Otiende had been exposed to national politics while he was still a teacher at Alliance High School. This was at a time when the political temperature was rising. He had observed the way the educated elite were being discriminated against by the white man. They earned lower salaries, lived in less attractive houses and were generally regarded as inferior. The emergence of a frustrated Western educated African elite gave the nationalist movements new impetus and resolve to fight colonialism. They became very vocal against the injustices. Otiende observes that one of the frustrating things then, was the absence of a forum through which the Africans could voice their collective or national concerns. The Local Authorities were limited and could not help. They actually helped the colonial authorities by ensuring that the grievances were contained at the local level. Africans did not have representatives in the Legislative Council. The colonial government had also proscribed national level political organisations and activity. It was a difficult period especially for the educated who understood the philosophy behind the colonial system. The colonial system condemned them to the periphery of governance. The educated were not trusted to hold senior positions in the government. In any case, Africans were closely supervised by their European bosses. The educated Africans were therefore determined to fight for their rights.

The Kenya African Union (KAU)

Sensing this change in the political climate, the colonial government nominated Eliud Mathu to the Legislative Council on 5th October

1944, hoping to cool down the political temperature. Mathu became the first African representative in the Legco. His nomination marked a small but important beginning of major political concessions to the Africans. It also gave Africans hope and encouragement that with consistent and determined pressure, more concessions would be forthcoming. Otiende and his colleagues saw the need to establish a colony-wide organisation to give Mathu support. A meeting was held in Nairobi and the Kenya African Union (KAU) was founded. Among those who attended this meeting were Eliud Mathu, J. D. Otiende, James Samuel Gichuru and Francis Khamisi. The formation of KAU was intended to unite Africans towards their own common cause and to foster their social, economic and political interests. It was to be used as a platform for political agitation and a forum for the articulation of general African grievances against the colonial system.

Otiende became an active member of KAU and was the party's chairman for the original Nyanza Province. All this time Otiende was still a teacher at Alliance High School. Any kind of political involvement was not encouraged in the school. He knew he was risking his teaching career and life as the colonial government was very ruthless while dealing with those opposed to its way of doing things. In 1945 the National Indian Congress in Kenya invited him to their annual conference in Mombasa. The conference was also attended by James Samuel Gichuru, Francis Khamisi and others. The meeting was reported in the *Mombasa Times*. This got Otiende in trouble with Carey Francis, the Principal of Alliance School where he was teaching. Otiende, however, was convinced that he was doing the right thing by identifying with the political aspirations of the vast majority of Kenyans. He had a difficult time as he now had a duty both to the school and to the party. The challenge was how to handle party matters discreetly without jeopardising his life and career. This did not deter him from serving the party. He would sneak out of school to attend to pressing issues of the party. He went to many parts of the country, including restricted areas, to sell the policies of the party to the people while also urging them to support Eliud Mathu. The most preferred mode of communication then was the word of mouth, which he effectively used to mobilise the support of the people. This method was preferred because it made it easy to conceal the identity of the leaders unlike now when leaders are hunted down through the Press.

Otiende's effort to unite Kenyans under one cause did not go unnoticed. The national leaders of KAU recognised these efforts and appointed Otiende the national secretary of the party, shortly after 1950, a position he held up to the Emergency period (1952) when the party was banned. He worked tirelessly to unite the people and to make KAU a powerful force in the colony. It was, however, not easy as the colonial government kept harrassing KAU members and officials. Otiende and the other party leaders did not give up after KAU was banned. They embarked on fresh efforts to agitate for the African cause. They repeatedly petitioned the colonial government for political and economic reforms, particularly a change in land policy and a more direct representation. It was towards this goal that in 1951, KAU submitted a memorandum to the Labour Colonial Secretary, James Griffith, during his visit to the colony, demanding *inter alia* direct elections in the place of nominations for African members of the legislative council. These petitions, however, continued to be largely ignored by the colonial government. Specifically, the colonial administration promised that there would be no land distribution or constitutional reforms that had been demanded by KAU. Otiende says that this decision did not quite surprise KAU given the determination by the colonial authorities to dominate the Africans. They however fought on. Their strategy at the time was to fight for one or a few concessions at a time. The issue of full independence was to come later.

While still the Secretary-General of KAU, Otiende was also an editor of a KAU paper, *Sauti ya Mwafrika*, Kiswahili for, Voice of the African. This paper was Otiende's own initiative in his tireless effort to unite the people of Kenya. He felt that there needed to be a medium through which people could be taught the benefits of unity.

THE FIRST CABINET: L to R (Front Row): James S. Gichuru, Kyale Mwendwa, Dr. Njoroge Mungai, Jaramogi Oginga Odinga, Mzee Jomo Kenyatta, Tom Mboya, Paul Ngei. (Middle Row): Joseph Daniel Otiende, Mbiyu Koinange, Achieng Oneko, Daniel arap Moi, Dr. Gikonyo Kiano, Samuel Onyango Ayodo, Charles Njonjo. (Back Row): Arthur Ochwada, Duncan Ndegwa, Joseph Murumbi, Bruce Makenzie and Lawrence Sagini.

As the Minister for Health, J.D. Otiende was privileged to host the 18th Session of the World Health Organisation (WHO) Regional Committee in 1968, which coincided with the 20th Anniversary of WHO. Here he is photographed with other dignitaries. He is seated in the middle.

At a function in the 1960s with cabinet colleagues, from left; Tom Mboya, Dr. Njoroge Mungai and Achieng' Oneko.

Addressing a public rally in a rural setting.

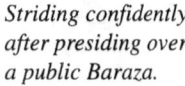

Striding confidently after presiding over a public Baraza.

Otiende in a jovial mood with the late President Mzee Jomo Kenyatta. In the middle is Achieng' Oneko.

As the Minister for Health, Otiende's duties went beyond the office and public functions. Here, he had visited the late Hon. James S. Gichuru, when he was hospitalised.

Otiende with Kenneth Matiba in the 1960s, when Matiba was a Permanent Secretary. Note Matiba's youthful features.

Otiende in a relaxed mood at a function in Vihiga.

At this function, Otiende was garlanded with roses as a sign of honour. With him is his wife, Martha Avoga.

The paper also helped to inform people of the events that were taking place in their country. Otiende's action encouraged others to start publishing more newspapers in an effort to unite and inform their people. Those who followed suit included Paul Ngei who started a Kamba paper. A paper in the Gikuyu language was also started. These papers were used by the emerging African elite to transmit to the remote African villagers the emerging anti-colonial messages. Although the readership was limited because of illiteracy, the papers proved very useful. They supplemented the verbal way of passing messages.

Armed Resistance

The period between 1947 – 1948 was when Africans had reached a point of being completely fed-up with the settlers who had taken their land. It was clear that Kenyans could never reconcile with British rule on matters of land policy. Their resolve in defence of a deep-seated attachment to the life-giving soil could not be over-emphasised. Thus, they were determined to resist any form of land alienation. The fear of losing more land made them feel insecure and want to resist all forms of injustice.

Failing to achieve their objectives by peaceful petition, they slowly moved towards more violent means. There emerged leaders from all over the country mobilising people in a bid to oust the settlers. Otiende felt that the situation could not have been as bad as it was if the colonial government had given some land to the Africans, as had happened in Rhodesia. He, however, thinks if this had happened, independence may have been delayed. Thus, due to the colonial government's stubbornness in land matters, African agitation took new twists and turns.

The people of Central Province became impatient over the land issue. Most of their land had been taken away by the European settlers. They decided to engage in 'bush' war.

In October 1952, the pro-government Senior Chief Waruhiu was assassinated in the process of rebellion. Sensing danger, the settlers forced the then Governor, Sir Evelyn Baring, to declare a state of emergency, which he did in 1952. However, having learnt some guerrilla tactics from their participation in the First and Second World Wars, Africans chose to fight from the forest, using Mount Kenya forest as their base. This saw the emergence of the Mau Mau Rebellion, whose main interest was participation by Africans in the running of the government and the land issue. Otiende explains that the aim of Mau Mau was to fight for the return of land to its rightful owners, the Africans, and also to demand that Africans be allowed to participate in the running of their country. Political independence as such was not the issue at the time. The initial demands focused on issues such as removal of discrimination, improvement of living conditions, the Kipande system and land alienation. Otiende explains this by the fact that initially the Africans did not think that the Europeans came to stay. It was after they realised that the colonial system was here to stay that the demand for independence was included in the list of grievances.

Once the Mau Mau war broke out, the British government intervened by mobilizing the best of its military and intelligence forces. By 1953 British Brigade Royal Air Force (RAF) squadrons, armoured cars and top intelligence officers had been sent to augment the brigades of the King's African Rifles (KAR). Henceforth, Africans were suppressed, harassed and thrown into concentration camps in a bid to control their activities. The rural areas saw the implementation of the 'villagization' policy in which people were moved into specially created villages (reserves) where they experienced all forms of torture that led to many deaths, maiming and even insanity. This policy was explicitly designed to break links between the Mau Mau fighters and their supporters and also to buttress the position of the loyalists. The Emergency, with its wholesale bloodletting and its savage campaigning, would rightly be viewed as the ultimate spasm of a society pushed to extremity.

At the beginning of the Emergency, all political organisations and activities by Africans were proscribed and leaders of these organisations detained. KAU, which represented the first national political party to be established in Kenya was proscribed on 8th June, 1953 because it had allegedly been used as a cover for Mau Mau. According to the then colonial secretary, Alan Lennox-Boyd, KAU had been the source of the pre-emergency militancy and violence. All its leaders were suspected to be Mau Mau sympathisers and were thus arrested and detained.

Mau Mau Sympathiser

Otiende was among the heroes who were arrested by the colonial government for their active involvement in the agitation for independence. He woke up on the morning of 20th October 1952 to find 13 askaris outside his house in Vihiga, where he had gone to bury his brother, waiting to take him away. Otiende's brother had died in the King George VI Hospital (now Kenyatta National Hospital) and Otiende had to travel to Vihiga for his funeral. The colonial administration was convinced that Otiende was a Mau Mau sympathiser and that he helped them by hiding them in his house. This allegation was true and Otiende was neither ashamed nor apologetic about it. He helped the Mau Mau who visited his area in present day Maragoli. He believed this was a very useful contribution to the struggle for independence. It also helped make the people of North Nyanza identify with people from other parts of the country who were fighting for the return of African land to the Africans with the eventual aim of achieving political independence.

He was locked up and subsequently put under house arrest where he remained for the nine years that the emergency period lasted. Being under house arrest meant that Otiende could not leave his house or receive any visitors. However, having had similar experiences in the past where his movements were restricted, he had discovered ways of overcoming this. His movements, for example, had been restricted when he was a teacher at Alliance High School when he served as a KAU official. He used these experiences to sneak freedom fighters into his compound and provide them with the assistance they required. This included food and water.

Looking back into the Mau Mau days, Otiende notes that the movement was country-wide though it has nowadays been *Gikuyunised* and presented to look like it was an exclusively Gikuyu affair. The fact of the matter, however, was that the Mau Mau and other freedom fighters were given support by people from all parts of the country where they operated. People in Nyanza and the whole of Western Kenya, for instance, supported the Agikuyu both financially and materially, in terms of food and other material resources. The Turkana of Northern Kenya assisted Mzee Jomo Kenyatta and others. Some freedom fighters sent their families to Nyanza to seek assistance. Otiende remembers having hidden Dedan Kimathi in his house and taking the latter's son to school when Kimathi was fighting in the forest. The fact that the movement originated in Central Province did not mean it was confined to the province, Otiende cautions. He says this should be known by all Kenyans, especially the youth who did not witness the events. He is sad that such an important event in the history of our country can be distorted for parochial political reasons. He urges the historians of this country to study the movement afresh and provide a more accurate picture of the Mau Mau.

Otiende's assertion that people who have written Kenya's history failed to recognise the other communities and individuals who helped in the struggle for independence, carries a lot of weight. Most people who call themselves Mau Mau today were not even born when the rebellion ended! Otiende feels that Kenyans have developed a very selfish attitude. Those who fought for the independence that we are now enjoying have largely been ignored. Most of them have been reduced to destitution, having lost everything they owned while fighting for independence. He gives the example of Bildad Kaggia who was very selfless but who the system has more or less left to die miserably. In comparison, Otiende says our Members of Parliament (MPs) have recently awarded themselves pension obtainable after serving the country for only five years – ignoring those who served the country for many (and painful) years. This is utmost selfishness, he observes, saying politics is about serving the people and not rewarding politicians. While Otiende acknowledges that politicians do an important job, he also notes there are other groups of people who do equally important jobs. According to him, the income gap between the MPs and other Kenyans should not be so glaring.

Analysing the performance of the Mau Mau, it is clear that they did not win the war so to speak. This was mainly because Emergency was declared before the leaders had effectively mobilized their forces. Though they fought some heroic battles, the Mau Mau could not hope to win for the movement was not strong enough either militarily or organisationally to withstand the combined imperial-colonial onslaught. The weapons used by the Europeans were obviously much more superior to those used by the Africans. However, the resistance portrayed by the Mau Mau succeeded in forcing recognition of African grievances and producing a genuine effort to deal with them. Political changes began to be instituted. Of these were the 1954 Swynnerton Plan and Lyttelton Constitution, both of which embodied new state policies. These, in various ways, reflected and shaped the underlying structural changes. The Swynnerton Plan was significant in that it transformed the agricultural policy by allowing Africans to hold title deeds to their land. There was also the introduction of the franchise for Africans in 1956 that overturned the administration programme for controlled development and set Kenya on the path to self-government.

From 1955, the colonial government lifted the ban on African political association. Henceforth, Africans were allowed to form political associations but only at the district level as an attempt to restrict their political activities at that level. The colonial government encouraged the Africans to air their political demands through these local associations. This was part of the divide-and-rule strategy applied by the colonial government to undermine the strength of the nationalists. Despite these constraints, the African elite that was then emerging, skilfully used its position to undermine European political influence and gain dominance that allowed it to move Kenya towards independence with great rapidity. They formed political organisations in virtually every district in the country. The first association to be registered was Argwing-Kodhek's Nairobi District African Congress. Others included Mombasa African Democratic Union, African District Association (in Central Nyanza), the Abagusii Association of South Nyanza District, the South Nyanza District African Political Association and the Taita African Democratic Union. In North Nyanza, Otiende formed the Abaluyia People's Association with him as the president. These associations became avenues through which the nationalists expressed their grievances, goals and aspirations. To date Otiende is still the president of the association though it has discarded its political nature and is now more of a welfare organisation. Different associations merged to form KANU and KADU respectively. This explains the fragility of KANU especially in the immediate post-independence year – it was an amalgamation of district parties.

In 1956 W.F. Coutts, who was the Chief Secretary, was appointed by the colonial government to head a commission to look into the possibility of enfranchising the Africans. Coutts recommended that Africans should be allowed to directly elect their representatives to the Legislative Council. The initial recommendation provided for eight African members of the Legislative Council. This in essence prepared a stage for the first ever general elections in the country.

In March 1957, Africans elected eight representatives to the Legislative Council to represent the eight regions into which the colony had been divided. The eight representatives were Daniel T. arap Moi (Rift Valley), Bernard Mate (Central), James Nzau Muimi (Ukambani), Tom Mboya (Nairobi), Oginga Odinga (Nyanza

Central), Masinde Muliro (Nyanza North), Ronald G. Ngala (Coast) and Lawrence G. Oguda (Nyanza South). This election marked a major watershed in the development of the Kenyan nationalist movement. It was also an important milestone in the politics of democracy in the colony. For the first time Africans were allowed to vote and to be voted into office. This concession by the colonial authorities also marked an important milestone in the constitutional development of the country. Nyanza North constituency had six candidates including Otiende, W.W. Awori and Masinde Muliro, among others. In the heavily fought battle, Otiende and the others lost to Muliro who emerged the winner. Having lost in the general elections, Otiende did not lose the spirit of serving his people and the country in general. Instead, the loss acted as a springboard into other avenues through which he could work for his country.

CHAPTER FOUR

THE EAST AFRICA COMMON SERVICES ORGANISATION

In 1961, Otiende was elected into the East African Legislative Council in what was then known as the East African Common Services Organisation (EACSO) that had been formed in the same year. EACSO was a regional body formed by the three East African states in an effort to foster regional co-operation. The organisation was the culmination of the British colonial measures to promote more unified administrative control over their East African territories. The EACSO was the precursor of the East African Community. But as colonialism was coming to an end and as Africans began to occupy responsible political positions, the three East African states began making deliberate efforts to develop new patterns of continental and regional co-operative arrangements. EACSO took over the general administration of the services that were common to the three countries; Kenya, Uganda and Tanzania. There were five committees of three ministers, one from each territory, to control the five groups of services, namely: Communications, Finance, Commercial and Industrial Co-ordination, Social & Research Sciences, Industrial Relations and Co-ordination of Labour. Later this ministerial committee system was replaced by a minister for East Africa from each state.

When Otiende was elected into the EACSO, he became the chairman of the Social & Research Sciences which incorporated fields such as research, education, health and agriculture. He was essentially the Minister for Education and Agriculture in the East African Legislative Council. Otiende served two terms in the East African Legislative Assembly. The first term ran between 1960 and 1963 and the second term was from 1964 to 1966. Thus, between 1963 and 1966, Otiende served as minister in the community and in the Kenya government. Otiende confirms that this kind of an arrangement was allowed at the time.

While serving his term, Otiende observed that very few East Africans had been trained in the field of medicine. The profession was then dominated by Whites. Furthermore, the few Africans who had been trained in the field had received their training abroad. In an effort to bring such training closer home, and also make it affordable, he arranged for the expansion of the Medical Training College at the present Kenyatta National Hospital and the medical training wing at Mulago Hospital in Uganda.

As far as education was concerned, Otiende was of the opinion that the development of the East African region as a whole depended on how well the East Africans themselves were equipped to handle the tasks that accompanied development. It was imperative that African education be made a priority if this goal of development was to be realised. It was towards this goal that Otiende arranged for the upgrading of Dar-es-Salaam University. Otiende was also in-charge of research centres such as those for leprosy and trypanosomiasis, among others. He considers these institutions as being of vital importance in the development of the countries of East Africa.

Otiende left the Social and Research Sciences sector and became the chairman of Transport and Communication. In this section also, he made tremendous changes that benefited the three countries of the East African region. For a long time the railway remained the backbone of freight transport, especially for the long haul traffic. Thus, knowing how important the railway was, Otiende came up with a programme to expand the lines so that the railway could serve more people in the region. In this programme the Uganda railway was extended from

Soroti to West Nile up to Arua and Gulu in Northern Uganda. In Kenya, the railway system was extended and joined the Tanzania lines. He was thus able to open up railway transport between the three countries. The railway lines were connected to water transport in Lake Victoria through Mwanza in Tanzania, Kisumu in Kenya and Entebbe in Uganda.

Otiende laments the deteriorating performance of the Kenya Railways and says something needs to be done urgently to revive the organisation. He hopes that this will be possible with the revival of the East African Community. Indeed, Otiende hopes that the transport infrastructure in general will be improved as it is key to socio-economic development. He blames the professionals for having let the country down, especially with regard to the building of roads. He says he cannot understand, for example, why a road that is professionally constructed should get potholes in under two years of construction.

He attributes the problems faced today to poor workmanship by the contractors and greed for money. This, he says, would not happen during the first few years of independence. People have come to place personal wealth above community or public service and so demand more money but do shoddy work. He also blames the problem on lack of effective supervision.

CHAPTER FIVE

INDEPENDENCE AND AFTER

KANU and KADU

Just before independence there emerged two national parties, the Kenya African National Union (KANU) and the Kenya African Democratic Union (KADU), formed shortly following the First Lancaster House Constitutional Conference held in 1960. The emergence of these two rival parties can be traced back to the political situation during the 1957 elections to the Legco. The colonial government had lifted the ban on African political activities but restricted the formation of political associations to the district level. Thus, in the 1957 election, African members of the Legco were not elected under the umbrella of a national party, which could have enhanced national unity. As a result local based politics emerged, thereby consolidating regional affiliations.

By the time the ban on national parties was lifted, a new system of African politics had been created where African political leaders depended on regional links. This facilitated the creation of increased differences amongst the elected African members to the extent that it was becoming difficult to maintain cohesion and agreement amongst them. Thus, they could not agree on several issues. Consequently, in July 1959 there was a split in the ranks of the African nationalists that produced two kinds of nationalism – one regionalist and the other centralist. One group led by Masinde Muliro, Daniel arap Moi and Ronald Ngala formed the Kenya National Party (KNP), and the other group formed Kenya Independent Movement (KIM) under the leadership of Oginga Odinga, Tom Mboya and Julius Kiano. It was this polarisation that led to the formation of KADU and KANU. The decision to permit the formation of colony-wide parties led to the establishment of KANU, in May 1960, by the adherents of KIM. The leaders of KNP declined to join KANU and formed a party of their own, KADU. The two parties were the result of amalgamation of the district-based political parties. This partly explains the fragility of the parties as each ethnic group tended to be more loyal to its leader as opposed to the national leader.

As a prelude to independence, elections were held at the national, regional and local levels. This was in line with the Majimbo constitution, which had been agreed on at the second Lancaster House Conference in London in 1962. The Majimbo constitution had been the brain-child of KADU which feared that a unitary constitution would give undue advantage to the bigger ethnic groups. This was really the main ideological difference between the two nationalist parties. The result was that the country was polarised along ethnic lines. KANU received most of its support from the so-called big communities, namely, the Agikuyu and the Luo, while KADU was supported mainly by the Abaluyia, the coastal people, the Kalenjin and Maasai communities.

Although the formation of these two political parties had polarised Kenyans along ethnic lines, it did not water down their resolve to wrestle independence from the colonial authorities. Otiende argues that there were many issues over which these ideological differences were underplayed for the sake of fighting the common enemy. Otiende was a staunch KANU supporter even though many of his Luyia colleagues such as Masinde Muliro and Martin Shikuku, were in KADU. He believed in the unity of Kenyans and thought that Majimbo would divide Kenyans unnecessarily. He saw no conflict between a unitary state and the protection of the interests of the smaller ethnic groups. What was needed, he believed, was the recognition that all Kenyans deserved to be treated equally. Kenya was not going to be the first country to have a unitary system of Government. Like many of his KANU colleagues, Otiende suspects that the members of KADU had European sympathisers who wanted their own protection after independence. These Europeans must have camouflaged their intentions behind KADU. Elsewhere in the continent similar fears were expressed by the federalists in Congo led by Moise Tshombe, who led his supporters against the unitarists under Patrice Lumumba. In the case of the Congo the real reason behind calls for federalism was the desire to protect the copper in Katanga region from people from other parts of the country. It was a question of struggle over resources. In the Kenyan case there was no particular natural resource that any region wanted to protect. Otiende still remains a firm believer in unitarism as a way of organising the management of the state. He is not in favour of the current suggestion that the country introduces Majimboism. Like many others who are opposed to Majimbo, Otiende argues for the strengthening of local government system and making the government and leaders more accountable to the people.

The split between KANU and KADU over the form and structure of government to be put in place threatened to delay independence. The issue was debated at the Lancaster House Conference in London at which the transfer of political power was discussed between the nationalists and the colonial government. The First Lancaster House Conference aimed to discuss the political destiny of Kenya. The conference, which lasted five weeks, agreed that Kenya required a new constitution. This marked a major turning point in the history of decolonisation of Kenya as it led to the enlargement of elected membership in the Legco with an African majority, thus paving way for independence under African rule. There were, however, disagreements regarding the type of constitution to be adopted. According to Otiende, the colonial authorities wanted to establish an apartheid system in which certain parts of the country would be for Europeans while others would be for the Africans – the kind of government that existed in South Africa then. This, according to Otiende, was the most detestable issue at the conference. The Second Lancaster House Conference was held in February 1962, a year before independence. In this Conference, which Otiende had the opportunity to attend, KANU was agitating for speedy election and the establishment of a date for independence. On the other hand, KADU wanted regionalism, as opposed to KANU's centralism, and also argued that the country was not ready for independence yet. The British government opposed KADU's emphasis on regional autonomy, but approved certain features of the party's plan, including a suggested bicameral legislature at the centre. This called for the establishment of a coalition government with equal representation. KANU decided to agree with the crusaders of Majimbo to adopt the Majimbo arrangement. It was, however, only a strategy to speed up the process of independence. Jomo Kenyatta was certainly not committed to this arrangement and made this clear soon after he assumed the presidency of the country. It is thus not suprising that federal arrangements in the constitution were abolised barely two years after independence.

Member of Parliament

During the independence election, Otiende was elected unopposed to represent Vihiga in the Lower House. This basically shows the respect the people of Vihiga had for him. He attributes this to the respect he had earned from the role he played in fighting for the rights of his people and the country in general. The people were confident that he was the man they wanted to represent their interests in Parliament. It also has something to do with his role in the African District Council. The people of Vihiga had a lot of expectations from their Member of Parliament especially on matters related to land. At independence many Africans were living as squatters, having been displaced by the settlers. Land alienation took place in different parts of the country and not just in Central Province. The Rift Valley Province and especially the present day Trans Nzoia District was among the areas affected by White settlement.

The colonial government that was handing over power to an African government realised this fact. Thus, at independence plans were underway to resettle all those whose land had been taken away. In the western part of the country the situation was equally devastating, as settlers had also displaced many Africans. To make matters worse the area was infested with tsetse fly, making it almost uninhabitable and the local leaders had to do something about it. Thus, to Otiende the biggest task was to resettle his people and also get rid of the tsetse flies. He obtained funds from the then governor and started clearing land where he resettled squatters. He was also able to contain the tsetse fly problem hence allowing people to farm peacefully. For this, the people of his area have always been indebted to him. He considers it one of his biggest achievements in his service to his people.

The May 1963 elections gave Kenya an African Government that was fully representative of the people and that was supported by an overwhelming majority in the National Assembly. On 1st June the country attained internal self-rule (Madaraka). Six months later, on 12th December 1963, full independence was achieved. The British flag, also known as the Union Jack, was lowered and the Kenyan flag raised to the jubilation of all Kenyans. The ceremony took place at midnight at the Uhuru Gardens along Langata Road. The venue was packed to capacity with happy Kenyans ready and eager to assume full responsibility for their destiny. Thus, after more than half a century of colonial rule there was a call for nation building at independence. This in essence required that men of vision be at the helm to define immediate and finite ends to be achieved by the state and device ways of meeting the requirements. Nation building had several components. It meant uniting the people and it was necessary in view of the fact that the colonial government had survived by pursuing a divide-and-rule policy.

As a cabinet minister, Otiende was always a busy man. In these four photos, he is seen performing various duties that fell in his docket.

Even today, Otiende is still active in social and political affairs especially at the local level. Here he is captured at a function with Minister Hon. Musalia Mudavadi and Hon. Yusuf Chanzu, the MP for Vihiga and an Assistant Minister.

Otiende with a guest at yet another function.

Above and below: Otiende is photographed at the swearing-in ceremony of the first cabinet. Below, Oginga Odinga is being sworn-in. Other cabinet colleagues in the picture include: Jomo Kenyatta, Tom Mboya, James Gichuru and Joseph Murumbi (partly hidden).

Otiende's wife, Mrs Martha Avoga Otiende

With his wife at a public function.

The policy had been first evident in the decision by the colonial government to restrict political organisation to the district level for most of the colonial period. This was intended to ensure that the people did not unite to fight the colonial masters. The district boundaries coincided with the ethnic groupings.

Nation building also meant restoring the dignity of the African people. The colonial government had undermined the dignity of the African people by treating them as sub-human beings. The racial discrimination that characterised the colonial system had been aimed at making the African feel inferior to the white man. The independent government felt it had the duty to restore the lost dignity. Reconstruction of the economy and enabling citizens to participate in the economy was also a part of nation building. This is why the Government emphasized on Africanization of the economy. At independence, most of the economy was under the control of foreigners. The Europeans controlled the industrial sector while the Asians controlled commerce. The achievement of the objectives was good for the country. However, it must also be noted that nation building as defined above was also politically important for those in power. The African leaders had to demonstrate to the people and the world at large that they were different from the colonial rulers. Consolidation of political power was thus part of the reason behind the nation building exercise. This should have been helped by the strong sense of nationalism that the struggle for independence had generated. Mzee Jomo Kenyatta understood the need to have capable people to assist him in this task of nation building. He was, therefore, very careful in selecting members of the first cabinet. However, the disintegration of the nationalist forces and coalition soon after independence did a major blow to the nation building enterprise.

Minister for Education and Culture

It was therefore not surprising that Otiende landed the portfolio of Minister for Education and Culture when Kenyatta named his cabinet in 1963. As already pointed out, Otiende was also serving as Minister in the East African Legislative Assembly. Kenyatta was confident that he could count on Otiende to bring positive changes in the education sector. At this time non-Africans were the ones providing most of the technical and professional services such as accounting, engineering and many others, almost exclusively. This is because colonial education in Kenya had been greatly unequal where African children had fewer educational opportunities than those of Europeans and Asians. Thus, at independence an insufficient number of Africans had been trained to assume major roles. Education, therefore, lay at the heart of the independent government attempts to foster social change and promote development. Therefore, from the onset of his career as the Education Minister, Otiende knew that political changes had to be made to expand the training of Africans for these responsibilities. He also realised that the future development of Kenya would require an increasing supply of trained manpower and a widening range of specialized skills. The main task then was to device an education programme appropriate to the manpower needs of the prevailing stage of development.

In this endeavour, Otiende was given the responsibility of drafting the Education Act in 1963. In preparing this Act, Otiende aimed at making it possible for Kenyans to use their energy and wealth in educating their children to get the relevant knowledge for their career requirements . He wanted a system that would expand the horizons and produce workers who could join the labour economy immediately. He recognised the need for an education system that would prepare Kenyans for the kind of jobs and lives they would encounter on leaving school.

The education system, like many other sectors of the country, had been subjected to racial segregation. Some schools were meant for Europeans only while others were reserved for Asians. The rest were for the Africans. A painful fact was that the facilities for Africans were of the lowest quality and standards as compared to those of the

Europeans and the Asians. They were also few and therefore inadequate. European schools included the present day Lenana, Kenya High, State House Girls, Jamhuri High School and Nairobi School. The Government saw the removal of racial segregation as the first major challenge in the education sector. Second was to improve the quality of education for Africans. Related to this was the need to increase the number of education facilities for Africans. As a Minister for Education, Otiende saw these as his first major areas of attention.

In tackling the priority areas though, Otiende faced many challenges. For instance, being at the initial stages of nation-building, there was a severe shortage of funds and other resources such as technical assistance. On 11th July, 1963, Otiende told Parliament that it would cost six million British pounds a year to finance a programme covering seven years of free education for all children. He went on to inform Parliament that such a sum of money was not immediately available. However, he added that this did not prevent the government from gradually moving towards seven years of free primary education as had been promised in the KANU manifesto. This did not dampen Otiende's spirit of wishing to provide relevant and affordable education to Kenyans. The impetus behind all this enthusiasm was probably an inherent principle that Otiende believed in – giving opportunity to others. The government sought foreign assistance from friendly countries, including Britain, the former colonial master. This assistance was made available to the country and it helped finance many projects that the country undertook as part of economic and social reconstruction.

The Ominde Commission

As part of the efforts to improve education, the government set up the first post-independence Education Commission in 1964 under the chairmanship of Professor Simeon Ominde. The Commission has since been known as the Ominde Commission. Otiende proudly says that he appointed Professor Simeon Ominde as Chairman of the Commission. He says that the appointment was based on his conviction that Ominde understood the country's education system well.

The main objective of the Commission was to come up with ways to make education relevant to the socio-economic and political needs of Kenyans and to open up education and training facilities for Kenyans. Its terms of reference included the survey of the existing educational resources and advising the Government on how to formulate and implement national policies for education that would express the aspirations and cultural values of an independent Kenya; take account of the need for trained manpower to facilitate economic development and other activities in the life of the nation; take advantage of the initiative and service of the regional, local authorities and voluntary bodies; contribute to the unity of Kenya; respect the educational needs and capacities of children; have due regard for the educational services; and provide for the principal requirements of adults. The Commission examined several aspects of the education system in the country and made a number of recommendations aimed at improving education. First, the Commission recommended a unified national education system in which there would be a common curriculum. The unification of the education system was important in view of the fact that the inherited colonial education system had separate schools for Europeans, Indians, Africans and Arabs. Few Africans went to school and those who did, received poor quality education as compared to the Europeans. It was imperative to change this system at the earliest opportunity as a way of reducing racial tensions. It would also demonstrate the determination by the independent government to break from the past.

The Commission recommended free education as a valid objective of educational policy. The commission stated that universal primary education was:

"so important a social service and ought to be freely available to all children and to be supported out of the revenue"

In order to expand education facilities, the Commission recommended the establishment of triple streams in primary schools. This was considered a cheap way of making more education places available. It is important to note that the majority of Kenyans were poor and could not afford the cost of education. Free primary education was therefore aimed at making it possible for the majority of the poor to gain access to education. In addition, Kenya, like many other African countries placed a lot of emphasis on education as a tool for the promotion of social and economic development. It was therefore important to make it more accessible to as many Kenyans as possible by giving it free. This policy worked very well as enrolment in schools rose considerably. In 1963, for example, there were 891,533 primary school pupils in the country. This rose to over 4.3 million in 1983. Expansion also occurred at the secondary school level. The enrolment rose from approximately 30,000 students to over 115,000 in 1969. This rose to over 500,000 in 1983. With time, however, budgetary constraints made it difficult to sustain this expansion. The government was forced to introduce cost sharing in schools. The cost of providing education is now shared between the parents and the government.

The Ominde Commission also recommended that the country should embark on the development of an adult education programme. This would be carried out through part-time classes to give those in employment a chance to go to school while still in employment. Indeed, the Commission urged the Ministry of Education to work out a scheme with the private sector to allow their employees time off to attend adult classes. The Commission was also concerned about Harambee schools that had sprung up partly as a result of encouragement by the government and partly because of the initiative of the communities themselves. The Commission insisted on proper control and planning of Harambee schools. It recommended that the government's attitude towards the self-help spirit with regard to schools needed to be guided by two principles: First, self-help had a permanent and valuable place in the provision of education. Second, government control had to be firm and complete, yet at the same time constructive. Moreover, it was necessary that this control be supported by the government and Members of Parliament. It was the same Commission that recommended that Harambee schools that did well be assisted by government in terms of providing teachers.

The emphasis on opening up education to as many Kenyans as possible was in line with the KANU manifesto which promised that the government would fight ignorance, disease and poverty. The policy influenced the building of several education facilities. These included primary schools, secondary schools and even post-secondary institutions. A number of Teacher Training Colleges were also built to provide teachers who would teach in the rising numbers of schools. Apart from the government-built schools and educational institutions, the people on their own initiative, constructed a number of self-help schools which were mostly secondary. They were meant to cater for those who were not lucky enough to gain admission into government schools, either because they did not meet the entry requirements or simply because of inadequate space in these schools. The communities had also been encouraged to build such institutions because the government promised to assist such schools by providing them with government-paid teachers. The result was actually overwhelming as many such institutions were built in different parts of the country. Thus while these schools fulfilled an immediate need, they created another problem – they became too many for effective management. The government simply could not supply teachers to all the Harambee schools as had been promised. This was going to make government lose credibility in the eyes of the citizens who expected the promised assistance. The government's answer to this problem was the decision to control the construction of such schools. The government called on the communities to ensure that the construction of such schools was planned or fitted within the country's education plan.

The need to open up more education facilities also led to the building of several commercial schools. Nowadays, they are referred to as private schools. They are of two kinds, namely, those built for the rich and provide high quality education and those that do not provide such kind of education. The present day Makini School in Nairobi would qualify as one built to provide high quality education while schools such as the former Kennedy High School in Nairobi fall under the latter category. The mushrooming of commercial schools presented the government with the problem of standards. In fact, on one occasion in 1963 Otiende, as Minister for Education, was asked in Parliament to issue a statement on the quality of these commercial schools. His response was that the government was considering reviewing the Education Ordinance in view of the large number of commercial schools that had suddenly appeared. He went on to declare that members of the previous Legislative Council had also expressed concern at the low standards of education in some of the private schools. The Minister informed Parliament that the schools were being investigated and reports received showed that it was still necessary to retain some control over the managers of the schools as a way of ensuring that they had the means and ability to manage the schools properly. He went on to say that the Ministry had to be satisfied that the schools would maintain a reasonable standard of education and provide an educational need. It is noteworthy that concerns about the quality of education offered by commercial schools continue to be raised to date.

Otiende also addressed the issue of the role of churches in the development of education in the country. Churches had pioneered the establishment of education in the country well before the colonial government got involved in this sector. After independence there arose the need to redefine the role of the Church and the other actors. The Minister observed that churches could no longer be regarded as the state's chosen agents for education because there were other interested parties, including the State itself. His argument was that church or religious-based education was not going to enable citizens build the nation. According to him, Kenya needed an all-round education that would prepare the youth for citizenship. This required more than just religious instruction or education with a focus on religious values. The country needed a balanced education that provided both religious values and beneficial citizenship values. Thus, the role of the Church in the provision of education was seen as complementing the state-centred education. The Church continues to be a major actor in the education sector even today. It may also be imperative to observe here that schools that are under the sponsorship of the Church have generally provided very high quality education over the years. These schools include Cardinal Otunga High School in Kisii, St Mary's Yala in Siaya and Precious Blood Riruta in Nairobi, just to mention a few. These schools have generally been very well managed with emphasis on student discipline.

As the Minister for Education, Otiende can therefore boast of having laid the foundations of a national education system that served the country for many years after independence. Many aspects of the present day education system are a carry-over from the recommendations of the Commission established during Otiende's tenure as Minister for Education. However, Otiende also remembers facing some drawbacks during his stewardship of the Ministry of Education. In particular he remembers an incident in which his cabinet colleague had attempted to replace a list of students who had been selected by the Ministry to travel to Bulgaria on Government scholarship with a different list without his authority or even knowledge. This unfortunate incident happened on the morning of 6th November 1963. Otiende was so infuriated by this incident that he promptly requested the Prime Minister to convene a cabinet meeting to discuss the matter. He raised a number of issues: First, he felt that the cabinet colleague who attempted to replace the list had undermined his authority as a minister. Secondly, he felt that this action undermined the principle of collective responsibility by which all members of the cabinet are bound by a government decision. He also wondered why the new list was prepared secretly.

Otiende also remembers having participated in the debates leading to the passing of the first Education Commission Act after independence. The Act was given assent on 6th February 1968. This Act, known as The Education Act 1968, aimed at promoting and regulating the progressive development of education in the country. More specifically, the Act addressed the following issues: Promotion of education; management of schools; registration of unaided schools; inspection and control of schools; examinations and diplomas; and establishment of the Kenya Institute of Education.

Otiende also participated in the committee that prepared the first post-independence Development Plan. His other colleagues in this task were Tom Mboya and Joseph Murumbi who were chosen to write the Development Plan because the cabinet trusted them and they had the experience. Such trust was hard-earned. Otiende had a track record of success in whatever he chose to do in the interest of his fellow Africans. His efforts did not go unnoticed and that was the reason he was chosen in the team that prepared the first Development Plan of the country.

Minister for Health and Housing

On 12th December 1964, Kenya became a Republic. The Prime Minister, Mzee Jomo Kenyatta, announced a sweeping reshuffle of the cabinet to launch the new republic. In this reshuffle, Otiende was named the Minister for Health and Housing. Immediately, Otiende set out to work hard as he had in the Ministry of Education. The health sector was also in a mess at independence just as the education sector had been. By 1962, for instance, there were only five provincial hospitals. The hospitals were at Kisumu, Machakos, Mombasa, Nakuru and Nyeri. They were augmented by a few mission hospitals operated by the Protestant and Catholic missionaries in Kenya. This implied that there was overcrowding in these health institutions, especially in the government hospitals since most Kenyans could not afford to seek medical services from the private hospitals. Otiende saw this as a major challenge to the country and to him as a minister.

He knew that overcrowding endangered the health standards of Kenyans. This, coupled with the fact that the available health facilities were over-stretched since they were serving large populations on very extensive areas, led him to take drastic measures in an effort to alleviate these problems. The long-term plan was to provide at least one health centre for every 10,000 people. Thus, for the next couple of years, Otiende embarked on a campaign of setting up health centres closer to the people. He ensured that enough money for this purpose was set aside during budgetary allocations. Thus, out of Otiende's efforts, health centres were built all over the country. In his home area Otiende remembers that his people used to walk very long distances to reach the nearest government hospital which was in Kisumu. To alleviate this problem he constructed the building currently housing Vihiga Municipal Council and turned it into a hospital. Otiende says that as a Minister, he had to balance service to the whole nation and service to his constituents without being seen to direct resources to his own area and neglecting others. The country had to rely quite heavily on foreign assistance to build health institutions. Otiende says at the time the donors had a lot of trust in the government. He attributes this to the fact that money given by donors for each project was fully accounted for.

This was also the period when the world was sharply divided between the two ideological blocks, namely, the East and the West. The East was communist and was led by the former Soviet Union and embraced all the Eastern European countries. The West, on the other hand, was capitalist and was led by the United States of America. It comprised virtually all the countries of Western and Southern Europe. Each of these ideological blocs wanted to extend its influence, if not control, over the countries of Africa that had just emerged from colonial rule. They were, therefore, more interested in giving aid as a way of extending this influence. Otiende observes that the government was well aware of this and attempted to minimise its effects. He says that the Government did this by accepting aid from both ideological camps. In his opinion, the decision by Kenya to become a non-aligned nation was also part of the strategy to avoid being swallowed by either of the two blocs. The policy gave the country the flexibility and freedom to choose when to support a particular bloc and when to oppose the same. This policy served the Government well. By the time he left, Otiende had helped build 250 health centres countrywide and 2 main hospitals, one being the Kinango Hospital in the Coast Province.

Looking around today, one realises that most hospitals, especially public ones, are built as one unit usually under one roof, so to speak. This is another of the significant contributions that Otiende made to the Ministry of Health and the country in general. The idea of having the whole institution as one piece was his personal initiative. This was done as a way of reducing cost and making movement easy. He strongly feels that cost should always be considered when doing Government work. He is saddened by the many uncompleted projects such as the buildings along Thika Road that were meant for the National Youth Service and the police quarters in many parts of the country. He wonders how the projects could have been initiated before proper budgeting was done.

Otiende felt obliged to provide affordable houses to the Kenyan population both in the rural and urban areas. He, therefore, planned to build houses for the different socio-economic groups of people. In this endeavour, he came up with plans to launch a revolution in house building ideas to give the republic a radical 'house-for-all' blueprint in one of the boldest housing drives yet seen in Africa. In his plan, massive cuts in housing costs were promised with the aim of bringing new homes within the reach of everyone. He referred to the houses as 'Jamhuri Houses'.

He believed that it was possible to build a rural version of the 'Jamhuri House' at the staggering speed of three days per house.

Nomadic communities would also benefit as he was also working on a more radical idea for a new house that would be folded up and carried from place to place. This plan, however, did not see the light of day. In Nairobi the plan seems to have worked. Many people were impressed to the extent that one of the city estates, Otiende Estate, was named after him. Nairobi's Jamhuri Estate is also a product of the plan initiated by Otiende. All these efforts by Otiende prove that he had the interests of Kenyans at heart.

Otiende observes that one of the major differences between the present crop of politicians and those of his time is that they saw politics as a service while the current crop of politicians see it as a career. Many go into politics to earn a salary and not to serve. This is one of the biggest problems in Kenya and Africa generally. Such leaders will be more concerned about their own interests and not those of the people. Kaggia, Odinga and Murumbi, who resigned their positions in government when they realised that the government was deviating from its policy of serving the people are cited as examples of selfless leaders of Otiende's time. These days, he says, it is very hard to find a politician resigning on matters of principle.

CHAPTER SIX

LIFE AFTER ACTIVE POLITICS

Even though Otiende served in the cabinet throughout his tenure as MP, in 1969 he lost the Vihiga parliamentary elections and decided to quit active politics. He noticed that things had changed from what they were during the first general election. His decision to quit was influenced by the fact that unlike in the past where people who sought to be elected had some experience, the people who now went for election did not have experience and Otiende felt that he would be out of place working with such people. Furthermore, he felt that the young generation that sought to be elected did not have the interest of the electorate at heart but were looking for jobs – politicians had turned politics into a career. He points out that most of the present day Members of Parliament see politics as a source of income and nothing more. This is an attitude that Otiende believes is not good for this country. He felt he could not fit in this kind of scenario and so he decided to quit and serve his people in other forums.

Retirement

Speaking about his retirement Otiende says:
"when I entered politics we were fighting for independence, later I was not only a Member of Parliament but a Cabinet Minister for many years. We had had our share, others had to now take over and do the rest".

He feels that a leader should not cling to power for too long as this would be detrimental to the political development of the country. He is therefore in favour of a limited term of office for presidents. He believes that serving for more than ten years would be counter-productive. People should leave office while still strong enough to serve in other capacities. It is time, he says, African political leaders became consultants to those who succeed them. If they die in office the country loses valuable knowledge. In this regard, Otiende has a lot of admiration and respect for former presidents Julius Nyerere of Tanzania and Nelson Mandela of South Africa. He observes that the constitutions of many African countries do not provide for limited term of office for presidents or Heads of States. This was partly due to the one party rule which did not envisage vacation of office by a serving president. Things are, however, changing and it is the hope of Otiende and others like him that appropriate constitutional changes that limit the term of office of African presidents will be introduced.

Constitutional Review

On the subject of constitutions and governance in Africa, and specifically the debate on the Kenyan constitution, Otiende is firm that the people must drive constitutional review. It is important at this point to make a distinction between constitutional amendment and constitutional review. Constitutional amendment simply involves or entails changing parts of the constitution. This process which has been done many times since independence, rightfully falls within the mandate of Parliament. However, a review of the constitution is tantamount to overhauling the constitution. This means re-writing or making a new constitution, a task that cannot be left to Parliament. To start with, Parliament is made up of politicians who see politics in everything they do. The constitution, however, must reflect the views of almost every segment of the society that it will eventually serve. Otiende is quick to point out that even the lawyers and other professionals represented in Parliament cease to see themselves as lawyers or even doctors while in politics. Instead, they see themselves as politicians. For this reason it is important to have non-practising politicians drive the constitutional review process. It must also be noted that politicians do not necessarily have the capacity to lead the process. Otiende asserts that the role of Parliament should be to provide the rules to be followed in reviewing the constitution. Parliament should also provide the funds by voting money to be used in the review process. The other role of Parliament is to approve the final document. The people, on the other hand, have the responsibility of determining the kind of constitution they want by expressing their views on various aspects of the constitution. These views can then be analysed by professionals and then given to lawyers to express in a legal language. This is really the most important role that lawyers have to play in the constitutional review process.

Otiende goes on to recommend that the Ghai Commission, while reviewing the country's constitution should not use the current constitution as a basis for reform. This, he says, is because the present constitution has been distorted through amendments that were not well intentioned. These amendments, he says, were meant to serve particular political interests and not the country as a whole. According to Otiende, the Ghai Commission should use the original Lancaster House Constitution, the Independence Constitution, as a basis for any debate on reviewing the current constitution. He believes very strongly that the original constitution had very noble provisions which could save this country from many of its current problems. He says for example, that the Local Government system that was envisaged by the original constitution is suitable today. We need to strengthen the local government system. The original constitution, for example, has provisions for the procedures of creating new local authorities which Otiende correctly points out have not been followed. As a result, he observes, we have local authorities that cannot serve the local people.

Similarly, he observes that the original constitution provides for procedures to be followed when altering boundaries. This again has not been followed especially when creating new administrative boundaries. He is of the opinion that many of Kenya's governance problems arise from the failure to adhere to the provisions of the constitution and selfishness on the part of leaders.

The Kenya Dairy Board

In May 1981, Otiende was appointed chairman of the Kenya Dairy Board for a three-year term that ended in 1984. This was a presidential appointment that he appreciates. He, however, points out that by the time he joined the Board as chairman, the organisation was already collapsing. He did everything he could to strengthen it but did not succeed. The failure of the Dairy Board is not unique. Many of the country's parastatals have actually collapsed due to poor management and political interference in the running of these organisations. The parastatal sector turns out to be a very parasitic sector in that the insolvency of many of the parastatals has forced the government to inject huge sums of money to keep them alive. They have become dependent on the state for survival. It is the poor performance of these organisations that convinced the donor community and particularly the World Bank and the IMF that such parastatals must be sold to the private sector. This is being done under the ongoing public sector reform that aims at, among other things, improving the efficiency and effectiveness of the public sector.

From KANU to FORD

Otiende was a member of the ruling party KANU up to the late 1980s. However, he says he felt let down by his party especially after he quit active politics. This was mainly because the post-independent government, both under President Jomo Kenyatta and President Moi, followed a strategy that was tempered by a growing authoritarianism and an unacceptable tendency to violence. From the late 1980s especially, KANU became increasingly authoritarian, over-riding public opinion, silencing the independent media and harassing critics and autonomous institutions such as the Church. He, therefore, decided to quit the party. This was at the time many Kenyans were not particularly happy with the one party rule that the ruling party advocated. There had emerged a clique of critics who were outspoken about the ills of the one-party rule. Among these people were Oginga Odinga, who soon came up with plans to organise an opposition to the ruling party. Otiende was approached by some people who wanted a person to help them organise a new party, a request he readily accepted, having been angered by the way KANU was carrying out its affairs.

The new party turned out to be the Forum for the Restoration of Democracy (FORD), which actually began as a pressure group. Thus, Otiende became one of the founder members of the pressure group FORD and later the chairman of FORD-Kenya in Vihiga District when the party split into FORD-Asili and FORD-Kenya. He attributes the split of the original FORD to lack of vision among some of the opposition leaders. Each of the leading opposition figures assumed they could become president simply because the Moi regime appeared weak. They did not understand the intricacies of politics and became blinded by their political ambitions. The split of the original FORD weakened the opposition. Otiende is of the opinion that if the original FORD had remained intact, the opposition would have taken over power in the 1992 elections.

Otiende says that the one-party system worked well in the immediate post-independent years. These were years when the country was generally unanimous about many fundamental issues affecting the country. The country agreed, for example, that national unity was needed, and that socio-economic development had to be given priority.

The need to fight against poverty, ignorance and disease was not disputed by anybody. There was also a general consensus that these nation-building efforts required the energies of every Kenyan. Political unity in the form of one party was considered as appropriate then. This was incidentally the same kind of argument advanced by virtually every African country irrespective of their ideological leanings. Thus, Tanzania, which under Nyerere was socialist, advanced similar arguments in defence of one party rule as did Kenya which, to all intents and purposes, was capitalist in orientation. It is also interesting that similar arguments were advanced by both the former British and French colonies.

With time, however, things changed as the challenges facing the government and the country became more and more complex. Among the changes he had in mind are the emergence of cleavages based on the failure of the government to pursue original party policies. The inclusion of former KADU politicians into the ruling party also created suspicions among the nationalists. There was mistrust and suspicion among the nationalists. In any case, many of the former KADU politicians did not completely abandon the ideological preferences that had divided them initially. Otiende seems to be saying that the time for one-party system had gone and the country needed to move into the multiparty era. He, in other words, does not regret the fact that he supported one party rule at some point in the political history of this country. He maintains that he did it at the right time.

However, owing to KANU's authoritarianism, opposition was viewed with a lot of hostility and force was used in trying to suppress it. Opposition leaders were harassed and some were even detained. Towards the end of 1989, the changing international environment, heightened by the collapse of Communism in Eastern Europe, encouraged the emerging opposition leaders to continue criticising the single-party rule and campaigning for the re-introduction of multiparty democracy. This, coupled with the external pressure the government was receiving from the donor countries and other lending institutions, left KANU and President Moi with no choice but to give in to the demands of multipartyism. This led to the repeal of Section 2 (A) of the constitution, making Kenya a multiparty state.

Even after joining the opposition, Otiende remained an unhappy man specifically because the opposition failed to live up to his expectations. Soon FORD was plagued by continual conflicts between the diverse set of men who constituted its leadership. The conflict crystallised into a cleavage that eventually led to a split. This split was basically caused by organisational ineptitude and, most of all, an ethnic struggle for the control of the party between the Luo and the Gikuyu leaders. This trend continued even after the original split and FORD-K further split into two factions, one led by Raila Odinga and the other led by Michael Wamalwa Kijana. Eventually Raila Odinga resigned from FORD Kenya and assumed leadership of National Development Party (NDP) while Wamalwa remained Chairman of FORD Kenya. Otiende had tried to reconcile the two leaders before the split but only succeeded in doing so for a short period. Angered by the in-fightings and splits, he decided to quit and watch. It needs to be pointed out that by the time Otiende quit politics, the style and approach to politics had obviously changed. Otiende may have found the going rather hard, which must have influenced his decision to quit.

After having retired from active politics Otiende still has the interests of Kenyans at heart. Currently, there is a growing disillusionment with the performance of the state and cynicism about the ruling party, KANU, leading to apathy and detachment among Kenyans. Otiende and the late Bishop Henry Okullu, among others, formed a pressure group called Friends of Democracy (FOD) with the aim of promoting and furthering democracy through educating the public on their rights and the responsibilities of their leaders, thus bringing Kenyans within the framework of conforming participation. FOD, a civil society initiative, is non-profit making and is not affiliated to any political party or religious body. It was formalised through the formation of the Institute of Civil Education and Development in Africa.

Regarding the succession debate, which Otiende has been following with keen interest, it is clear to him that though a lot has been said, it is still not clear how succession will take place come the end of President Moi's term. In a bid to ensure that this is done as peacefully as possible, FOD devised possible ways of choosing the next president. He could not disclose to us these plans. It is, therefore, the aim of the pressure group to see to it that change of government is done peacefully.

In his retirement, the father of eight, four boys and four girls, lives with his wife, Martha Avoga, since his children, now all grown up, live away from home. Otiende's first-born is a daughter who has recently retired as headmistress of a secondary school. His second-born, a son, is a retired aircraft engineer with Kenya Airways, followed by another son who is currently a university lecturer in Maryland, USA. The fourth child, a daughter, works with the government as a public health officer. The fifth is a son and a graduate of Egerton College. He studied veterinary medicine and has worked as a veterinary officer with the government since graduating. The sixth child unfortunately died and was followed by twins, both of whom work in the medical profession as physiotherapists. The last-born is a girl, currently holding the position of Deputy Secretary in the Ministry of Home Affairs, Heritage and Sports. Only one son lives in his compound.

Traditional Medicine

Otiende does some research on traditional herbal medicine while at the same time updating himself on trends in modern medicine. His profound interest in medicine began early in his school days. He worked hard in school to ensure that he got a chance to study medicine. This dream was fulfilled when he was admitted in Makerere to study medicine. However, as already stated, teaching was the 'in-thing' those days and although Otiende was not interested in studying education the elders in his village decided that they wanted their son to become a teacher. As tradition demanded, Otiende could not go against their wish. Thus, he quit medicine after studying for some time and concentrated on education. This, however, did not make him lose interest in medicine. In his own way he continued learning more on his most preferred field, medicine, both modern and traditional.

So far he has discovered that diabetes has become a problem in Maragoli. He attributes this to the Western diet that the people are exposed to these days. The educated people have abandoned traditional foods in favour of Western foods. This, according to Otiende, is a major cause of the problem. The traditional foods he has in mind include millet, cassava, sweet potatoes, porridge, and locally grown vegetables such as *kunde* (cowpeas leaves). Modern medicine is mainly used to bring the disease under control. Otiende, however, has discovered a concoction prepared from natural herbs, that he claims can cure, not only diabetes, but also asthma and other fevers. He gives this traditional herbal medicine to those who seek them free of charge. This gesture of generosity has served to make Otiende more popular among his people.

Otiende asserts that Africa is rich in medicinal plants which should be exploited for the development of medicine. He is worried that foreigners claim credit for many scientific developments that have their origins in Africa. He blames this on the tendency of Africans to trust Europeans too much even after the latter demonstrated that they are not always as trustworthy as the rest of the world tends to think of them. In this regard, Otiende believes that the struggle to decolonize the minds and attitudes of Africans remains a challenge. There is need to respect our African culture and values and to reject those Western values that are destroying the good things in Africa. This, he hastens to add, is not a racist position. Indeed, he says, we should respect people of all races, and we must also admit that cultural relativism is a good thing.

Still in the field of medicine, Otiende is of the opinion that Kenya has the potential and capability of developing a cure for AIDS. His position is based on the recent developments in the field, which saw the emergence of the drug KEMRON, and also in the recent research that Kenyan scientists carried out in conjunction with British scientists in developing an HIV vaccine. Having knowledge in human anatomy, Otiende suggests that scientists interested in developing a cure for AIDS should in fact base their studies on the sickle cell, which he believes is the key to getting the cure. In an AIDS conference he attended in his area, Otiende aired his view that the cure for AIDS will come from Africa. He also believes that a change of diet can go a long way in helping to curb AIDS.

Promoting Democracy

On the political scene, Otiende has not been quiet or indifferent even in retirement. Looking at the political climate of the country, he feels that a lot is still left to be done especially in promoting democracy. Though the political leaders of this country claim to be committed to the doctrines of democracy, practically very little is being done towards this goal. Otiende's efforts to unite people always transcended Kenya's national borders. He joined the Capricorn African Society. In Kenya the Society had been started in 1948 with the aim of harmonising the relationship between the Whites and the Africans. This was mainly because it was believed that the Blacks and Whites needed each other in the task of building a prosperous and peaceful Kenya. The Capricorn contract stood for the establishment of true stability and confidence, abolition of racial discrimination, gradual progress towards self-government and the establishment of a common citizenship for all Kenyans. Otiende became the member of the society in his region. Together with Mr. Richard Hughes, he tried to reconcile the Blacks and Whites of South Africa. This is mainly because he believes that Africans cannot progress without unity.

Otiende the Author

Otiende found time during the struggle for independence to engage in the writing of a book on the Luyia community. In 1949 he published a book, *Habari za Abaluyia*. The book, which was published by Eagle Press, is the first volume in the series, Customs and Traditions in East Africa. The series aimed at recording and preserving the oral traditions of the people of East Africa. There was danger of culture dying out because it was no longer effectively being handed down from the elders to the younger generation due to modernity and its consequences on family cohesion and stability. The book by Otiende aims at giving young Africans as well as members of the other races an opportunity to study history, traditions and customs of the Abaluyia. This would help in making it possible for the people to have a more balanced view of life in view of the complexities of modern life and values.

In his foreword to the book, one of his teachers at Makerere, Mr R.A. Snoxall, who was at the time the Acting Director of Education in Uganda, comments:

> It was soon quite obvious to us, his teachers, that his thoughts upon the evolution and development of Africa and its peoples were of an unusual depth and clarity and that he had a great gift of seeing events and trends in their true perspective (Otiende, 1949).

He goes further to say Otiende's view that there were great unifying possibilities about a language like Oluluyia, whose form and vocabulary was so widespread, has already been vindicated. The evolution of a common language and a common orthography have done perhaps more than anything else to unify the various sub-tribes into the Abaluyia of North Nyanza. Snoxall compares Otiende's book with that of Monica
Hunter, *Reaction to Conquest*, written on Pondo-land and its peoples. Otiende's book provides, in graphic form, the historical and geographical background, which is necessary in order that the

Abaluyia may be properly understood. In the book, he begins by describing the geographical location of North Nyanza and the histories of the different "tribes" found therein. He then proceeds to give the customs and traditions that were practised by the inhabitants of North Nyanza.

Otiende says that initially, the region occupied by North, Central and South Nyanza was known as North (Kavirondo) Nyanza. But the word "Kavirondo" could not be clearly identified with any tribe in Nyanza. Thus, on 1st September 1948, the government gave in to the pressure by the people who were agitating for a change of name and agreed to change the name to North, Central and South Nyanza. The change of name, however, created a new problem, namely, the name to be given to the inhabitants of North Nyanza. The people of South and Central Nyanza were predominantly Luo, although there is a sizeable number of Avaloogoli in Migori District of former South Nyanza District.

A number of new names were floated. One such name was "Bantu Kavirondo". This was, however, rejected as inappropriate since not all inhabitants of the area were Bantu. Secondly, there were other Bantu communities in Central and South Nyanza. It was in the course of searching for an appropriate name that the people of North Nyanza came up with the name "Abaluyia". They decided to use a common name because even though there are a few differences in their dialect, they realised that they were from a common origin. The book by Otiende was awarded the Swahili authorship prize by the Inter-territorial Language Committee.

Today, Otiende is doing an in-depth history of the people of Kenya, studying their origin and migration. He believes that so much was left out while writing the migration history of the Kenyan peoples, some of which is being revealed now. Specifically, he feels that much was missed in writing the Abaluyia history. Historians have variously argued that one of the biggest problems of dealing with the history of the Abaluyia as one group is that, each of the seventeen sub-nations that inhabit Buluyia has its own story of origin, migration and settlement – that each component claims a different origin and ancestry. Thus, historians have, more often that not, treated each sub-nation as a separate entity. Otiende, however, feels that it is quite wrong to refer to the Abaluyia as a heterogeneous ethnic group. He argues that the Abaluyia were originally known as *Abananda*, meaning one family. He is writing, therefore, to correct the mistakes made by historians, most of who are not even Kenyans.

Otiende takes his Christian belief with a lot of seriousness, having been brought up in a Christian family. His father who, having been a preacher, had wide knowledge of the Bible passed on this valuable virtue to him. In his local church, Otiende is an advisor to some of its organisations. He was also part of the panel of Logooli experts that worked on an Olulogooli Bible translation.

Cultural Activities

Otiende strongly believes in the value of culture. To him culture plays a critical role in the creation of a cohesive and harmonious community. He views culture as a source of progress both for the individual and society as a whole. This is because, according to him, culture is the vehicle through which societal values are inculcated in the individual and society. This helps in shaping an individual's and community identity. He observes that according to the Luyia culture, only the positive values are emphasized through cultural education while the negative ones are discouraged. The Abaluyia, he says, have different ways of discouraging negative values among its youth and the community generally.

It is because of the positive role played by culture that Otiende is proud to be associated with the annual Maragoli Cultural Festival. He is currently the chairman of the Vihiga Cultural Society that organizes the Maragoli Cultural Festival. This society has a constitution which Otiende helped draft. In fact many of Otiende's views on culture are

evident in the constitution of the society. The society has a council of elders. The duties and functions of this council include:
- (i) To act as the guardian and custodian of the traditions and cultural values of the Society and the community at large.
- (ii) To function as the supreme authority and final arbiter in matters of Logooli customs and traditions.
- (iii) To arbitrate in disputes arising from breach of customs and taboos.
- (iv) To review through extensive consultations, traditional practices and customs that appear out of tune with current social and legal realities and pronounce itself on the matter.
- (v) Plan, coordinate, oversee, harmonize and advise on matters of Logooli circumcision ceremonies and rites of passage.
- (vi) Advise and counsel the youth on matters of traditional etiquette, good manners and acceptable conduct.
- (vii) Liaise with elders from other neighbouring and distant communities that have cultural and matrimonial relations with Logooli with a view to harmonizing the relations and practices.

Some of the objectives of the Vihiga Cultural Society as stated in the constitution are:
- (i) To revive, develop and sustain a common cultural consciousness, cultural values and institutions among the Avalogooli.
- (ii) To organize cultural talks, symposia, music, dances, drama, exhibitions, displays, games and sports with a view to promoting common cultural consciousness, values and enjoyment among members of the community at large.
- (iii) To collect, document, store and preserve intellectual material, cultural items and records relevant to Logooli culture for the benefit of the members of the community at large and posterity.
- (iv) To encourage cultural exchanges with other communities and societies.

(v) To publish and disseminate literature which highlights Logooli culture, history and moral values.
(vi) To research, develop and standardize Logooli language and its orthography.
(vii) To encourage, sponsor and promote youth participation and involvement in the Society's activities with a view to encouraging cultural education, transfer and sustainability.
(viii) To promote and support authorship of Logooli books and other literary materials among Avalogooli.
(ix) Liaise with the relevant authorities of the government with a view to incorporating Logooli literature and cultural materials in the school curriculum.

Otiende also believes in cultural relativism and is opposed to the imposition of one culture over another. This is why he cautions against globalization, which he views as an attempt to impose Western culture on non-western societies, Africa included. He is of the opinion that Africans should resist western values that undermine their positive cultural values. This, he says, does not go against his belief that culture is dynamic and is bound to change in response to changes in one's wider environment. This, however, should be natural and not imposed, nor should it be legislated.

Otiende is very proud of the cultural festival and hopes that other communities will emulate what the Avalogooli are doing to preserve their culture. This is very important at this time when global forces threaten to erode our cultural values. Deliberate efforts need to be initiated to preserve positive African cultural values and practices, and the Maragoli Cultural Festival should be seen against this background.

CHAPTER SEVEN

CONCLUSION

Without doubt, Joseph Daniel Otiende is one of the nationalists who spearheaded Kenya's struggle for independence. He was also among the first cabinet ministers who laid the foundation of the first government following the attainment of political independence in 1963. He was the first Minister for Education and later became the Minister in-charge of Health and Housing. Otiende also served in the East African Legislative Council. After an honourable retirement from politics, Otiende continues to be active in local level development activities. He is for example, actively involved in the Vihiga Cultural Festival, an annual cultural event that attracts the participation of the President and high ranking public officials not just from Maragoli but from all over the country. The cultural event is a good demonstration of the way in which Africans can preserve their cultural heritage. Otiende is proud to be associated with this event.

Despite this very active life, many Kenyans hardly hear about Joseph Daniel Otiende. Indeed, many people do not know if he is still alive, precisely because they do not hear about him, especially in the press. Since quitting politics in 1969 he has kept a very low political profile. He is one of the few Kenyan politicians who quit active politics on principle. He quit politics because he believed that the party he loved so much had betrayed the people of Kenya and he did not wish to be associated with it any more. He also felt the opposition parties did not have much to offer to Kenyans and his experience with the

FORD wrangles showed him that present day politicians are driven by selfish considerations. Another reason for his quitting active politics was because he thought it was time for younger people to play their role. Nevertheless, he still gives a lot of support to his MP.

The decision to quit politics has paid dividends for Otiende. The most significant of these is the respect accorded him by his people and indeed many other Kenyans. Otiende continues to be consulted on a wide range of issues by a number of people from his community. Thus, the decision to quit politics was good in that it helped him avoid being embarrassed by the ruthlessness of Kenyan politics and hence retain his position of honour in society.

We have tried in this book to highlight Otiende's contribution to the political and other aspects of the country's development. Our study revealed that Otiende is indeed a humble man. This humility is quite evident from the way he talks and treats people who visit his home. It is even more evident from the type of home and house he owns and lives in. Unlike his contemporaries, Otiende lives a very modest lifestyle in the village. He prefers a simple life. This kind of politician is rare in Kenya. Most of the current leaders would rather live luxuriously while the common man suffers. Otiende does not think this is necessary or even desirable. Leaders, he believes, must not be seen as far removed from the people they lead.

Otiende remains a well informed person and has knowledge of very current scholarly publications. It is also noteworthy that at his age, he continues to draft very important documents for his community.

His ability to discuss current global as well as domestic political and economic issues shows he has kept abreast of developments by relying, not just on newspapers, but also by reading books and discussing issues with the many people who visit his home.

Otiende has interests in music, culture and drama. This perhaps explains his active involvement in cultural activities in his home district, the Vihiga Cultural Festival.

BIBLIOGRAPHY

Crowley, J. N. **Colonial Policy and Nationalism in Kenya 1952-1963,** Ph.D Thesis.

Furedi, F. (1989), **The Mau Mau War in Perspective,** Heinemann Educational Books, Nairobi.

Gertzel, C. (1970), **The Politics of Independent Kenya 1963-8**, Heinemann Educational Books, Nairobi.

Gichuru, H. B. N. (1976), **Parliamentary Practice in Kenya**, Transafrica Publishers, Nairobi.

Mushelle, J. S. (1980), **The Control of Local Government Authorities**, M.A. Thesis, University of Nairobi.

Ogot, B. A. and Zeleza, T. "Kenya: The Road to Independence and After". In Gifford and Louis W.R (eds.), (1988), **Decolonisation and African Independence: The Transfer of Power, 1960-1980**, Yale University Press, Yale.

Ogot, B.A. and Ochieng, W.R. (eds.), (1995), **Decolonisation and Independence in Kenya: 1940-1993**, East African Educational Publishers, Nairobi.

Otiende, J.D. (1949), **Habari za Abaluhyia**, Eagle Press, Nairobi.

Oyugi, W. (1978), **Local Government and Development in Kenya,** Sussex University, Institute of Development Studies (Discussion Paper).

Sifuna, D. (1990). **Development of Education in Africa: The Kenyan Experience.** Initiatives Publishers, Nairobi.

The Economic Development of Kenya, Report of an Economic Survey Mission, 1962.

Throup, D.W. and Hornsby, C. (1998), **Multi-party Politics in Kenya: The Kenyatta and Moi States & the Triumph of the System in the 1992 Election**, East African Educational Publishers, Nairobi.

Wagner, G. (1939), **Changing Family among the Bantu Kavirondo**, Oxford University Press, London.

Republic of Kenya (1964), **The Ominde Commission Report 1964**, Government Printer, Nairobi.

The Constitution & Rules of Vihiga Cultural Society.

www.ingramcontent.com/pod-product-compliance
Lightning Source LLC
Chambersburg PA
CBHW070741230426
43669CB00014B/2538